ATTACK OF THE...

BEASTLY BACTERIA

By William Anthony

Enslow
PUBLISHING

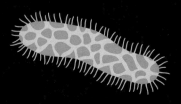

Published in 2021 by Enslow Publishing, LLC
101 W. 23rd Street, Suite 240,
New York, NY 10011

Cataloging-in-Publication Data

Names: Anthony, William.
Title: Beastly bacteria / William Anthony.
Description: New York : Enslow Publishing, 2021. | Series: Attack of the... | Includes
glossary and index.
Identifiers: ISBN 9781978519916 (pbk.) | ISBN 9781978519930 (library bound) | ISBN
9781978519923 (6 pack)
Subjects: LCSH: Bacteria--Juvenile literature.
Classification: LCC QR74.8 A584 2020 | DDC 579.3--dc23

CPSIA compliance information: Batch #BS20ENS: For further information contact Enslow Publishing, New York, New York at 1-800-542-2595

PHOTO CREDITS

All images courtesy of Shutterstock. With thanks to Getty Images, Thinkstock Photo and iStockphoto.

Used throughout (including cover) – chekart (background), Sonechko57 (slime), VectorShow (microbe characters), Alena Ohneva (vector microbes), Olga_C (circle image frame). Used throughout (excluding cover) – Photo Melon (clipboard), Lorelyn Medina (scientist characters). P4–5 – Sebastian Kaulizki, nobeastsoffierce, p6–7 – Cortyn, Tatiana Shepeleva, p8–9 – Kateryna Kon, New Africa, p10–11 – Kateryna Kon, Kakigori Studio, p12–13 – Casezy idea, Voyagerix, p14–15 – drsnaut, ElRoi, VectorShow, p16–17 – Scott Nelson (flickr.com), Bhai (wiki commons), p18–19 – Kateryna Kon, Artemida-psy, dapoomll, p20–21 – Kateryna Kon, yatate, p22–23 – Dragon Images, Monkey Business Images

CONTENTS

Words that look like <u>this</u> can be found in the glossary on page 24.

TRICKY WORDS

BACTERIUM = one bacterium
BACTERIA = many bacteria
BACTERIAL = having to do with one bacterium or many bacteria

TINY TERRORS

What is the smallest thing you can think of? Is it so small that you can't even see it? This is how small microorganisms are.

"Micro" means tiny. "Organism" means a living thing.

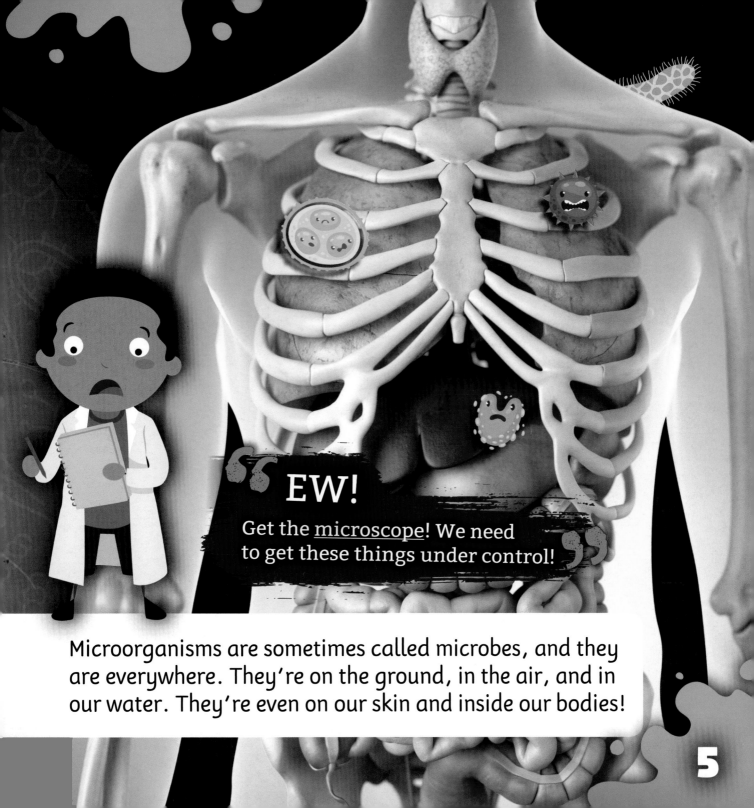

EW!

Get the <u>microscope</u>! We need to get these things under control!

Microorganisms are sometimes called microbes, and they are everywhere. They're on the ground, in the air, and in our water. They're even on our skin and inside our bodies!

BEASTLY BACTERIA

Bacteria are a type of microbe. They are alive, and some bacteria can use their taillike parts to swim.

Does that mean they can swim inside our bodies?

WOW!

Bacteria can be found all over the world. Some bacteria have <u>adaptations</u> that help them live almost anywhere.

We can't even move to the desert to escape them? Great.

Many bacteria are useful to the planet and to us. Bacteria help plants grow and help us break down food in our stomachs.

"Thank you, good bacteria, for my **happy tummy.**"

8

Other bacteria can be bad for us. If some types of bacteria get into our bodies and into our blood, it's not good news.

"Watch out!

The bacteria are on the loose!"

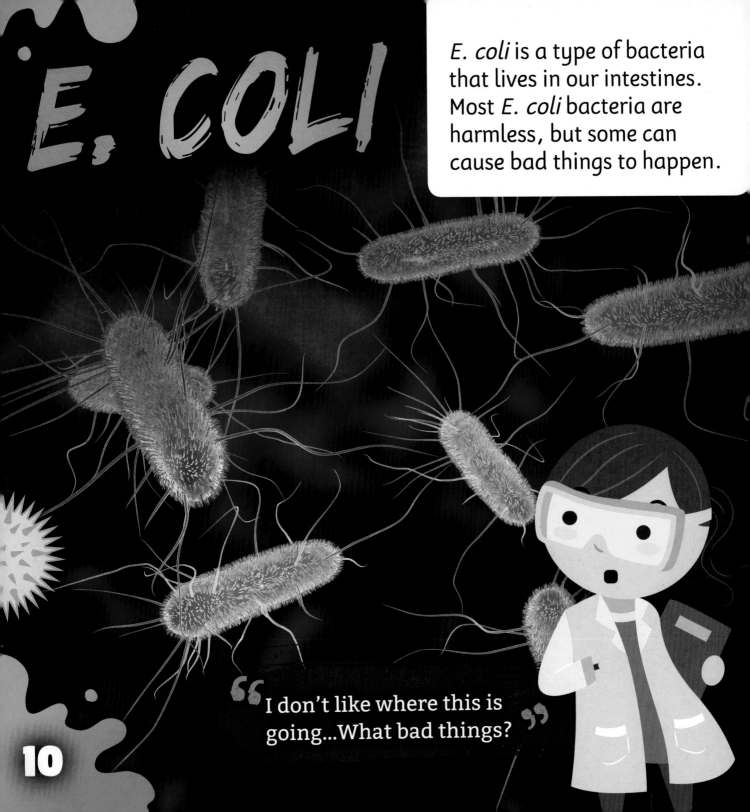

E. COLI

E. *coli* is a type of bacteria that lives in our intestines. Most *E. coli* bacteria are harmless, but some can cause bad things to happen.

"I don't like where this is going...What bad things?"

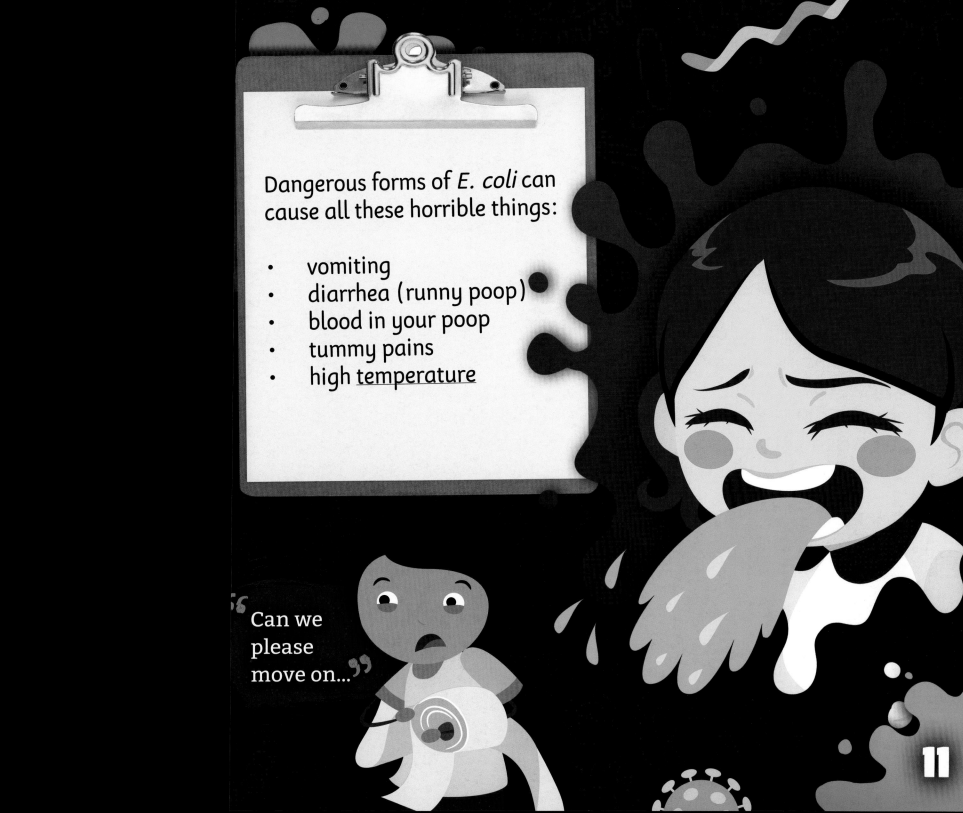

BLACK HAIRY
TONGUE

Bacteria can do all sorts of strange things to our bodies. A buildup of bacteria in our mouths can cause something called black hairy tongue.

These bacteria are the worst! Somebody save us!

> Brushing your teeth at least twice a day helps to avoid black hairy tongue.

Black hairy tongue is actually harmless. It just causes your tongue to look like it has black hair on it.

13

EYE
INFECTIONS

Bacteria can affect us and other animals in the same ways. Your eyes can get some of the same bacterial <u>infections</u> as your pet's eyes.

Oi! Bacteria!
You leave Gumbo alone!

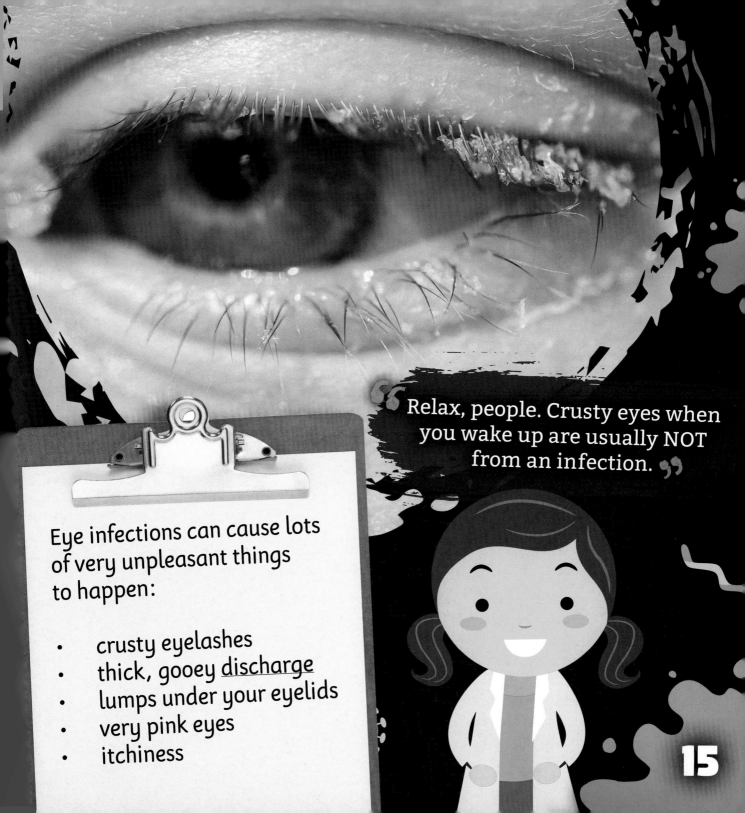

Relax, people. Crusty eyes when you wake up are usually NOT from an infection.

Eye infections can cause lots of very unpleasant things to happen:

- crusty eyelashes
- thick, gooey <u>discharge</u>
- lumps under your eyelids
- very pink eyes
- itchiness

15

CROWN GALL

Bacteria aren't fussy. They can launch an attack on plants as well as on us. Crown gall is a bacterial <u>disease</u> that can kill plants.

"Plants too?
I'm done. I want to go home."

"The end is near, folks.
The bacteria have taken over."

Crown gall causes knobbly, round growths around the stems, roots, trunks, or branches of the plant. This can lead to the death of the plant.

MRSA

MRSA is a type of bacteria that can't be beaten by many common <u>antibiotics</u>. Some people call it a superbug.

"Wait, hold on a second. Can't be beaten?
We're DOOMED!"

MRSA can cause some nasty effects if it gets under your skin:

- boils filled with pus
- <u>abscesses</u> filled with more pus
- <u>carbuncles</u> filled with even more pus

"SO MUCH PUS!"

19

BUBONIC PLAGUE

One of the most famous bacterial infections of all time killed millions of people in the 1300s. Have you ever heard of the bubonic plague?

" The bubonic plague is also known as the Black Death. It doesn't sound fun. "

It causes black lumps called buboes to grow under the armpits, on the neck, and around the <u>groin</u>. They are filled with blood and pus.

"The bubonic plague still exists, but we can cure it easily now. Panic over!"

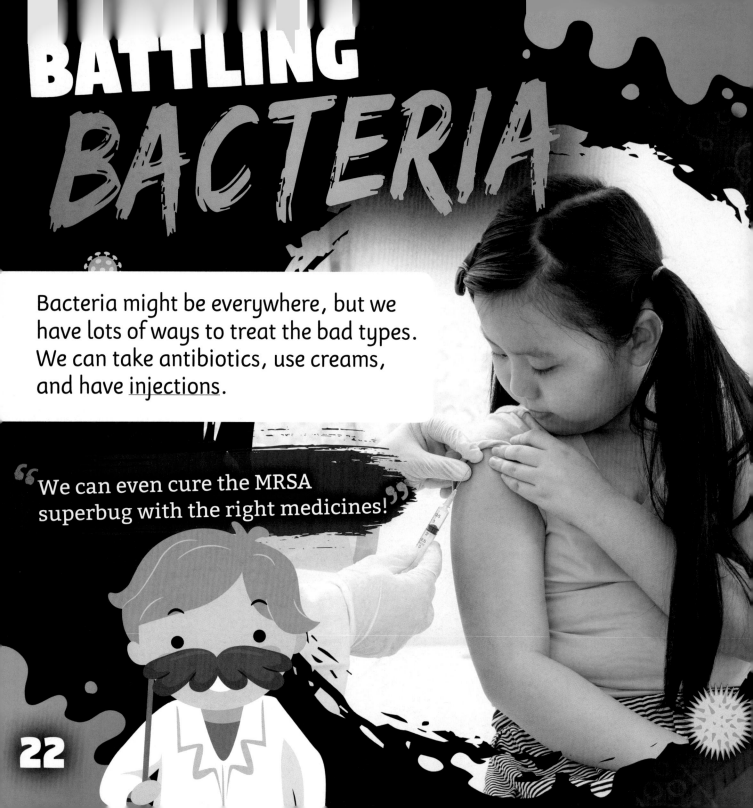

BATTLING BACTERIA

Bacteria might be everywhere, but we have lots of ways to treat the bad types. We can take antibiotics, use creams, and have <u>injections</u>.

"We can even cure the MRSA superbug with the right medicines!"

We can stop bacteria from <u>spreading</u> too. We can wash our hands, keep ourselves clean, and not share towels, clothes, or bedding. The battle against bacteria has begun!

This is MY towel. MINE. Stay away from it. "

23

GLOSSARY

abscess	painful swelling under the skin that is filled with pus
adaptation	a feature in a living thing that makes it better suited to live in a particular place
antibiotic	a medicine that is used to kill harmful bacteria and cure infections
carbuncle	a very large, painful swelling under the skin that is filled with pus
discharge	liquid that comes from a part of the body that is infected
disease	an illness that causes harm to the health of a person, animal, or plant
groin	the area where the legs meet the rest of the body
infection	illness caused by dirt or microbes getting into the body
injection	a measured amount of liquid medicine that is put into the body with a needle
microscope	a piece of scientific equipment that makes things look many times bigger
spreading	moving around from place to place to affect a larger area
temperature	how hot or cold something or someone is

INDEX